BEHIND THE SCENES
BIOGRAPHIES

WHAT YOU NEVER
KNEW ABOUT

>>> ———————————— <<<

BEYONCÉ

by Mari Schuh

CAPSTONE PRESS
a capstone imprint

For Aleyna

This is an unauthorized biography.

Published by Spark, an imprint of Capstone
1710 Roe Crest Drive, North Mankato, Minnesota 56003
capstonepub.com

Library of Congress Cataloging-in-Publication Data
Names: Schuh, Mari C., 1975– author.
Title: What you never knew about Beyoncé / by Mari Schuh.
Description: North Mankato, Minnesota : Spark, an imprint of Capstone, 2023. | Series: Behind the scenes biographies | Includes bibliographical references and index. | Audience: Ages 9–11 | Audience: Grades 4–6 |Summary: "She's not called Queen B for nothing! What makes Beyoncé a megastar? High-interest details and bold photos of her fascinating life will enthrall readers"—Provided by publisher.
Identifiers: LCCN 2022022115 (print) | LCCN 2022022116 (ebook) | ISBN 9781669002918 (hardcover) | ISBN 9781669040538 (paperback)| ISBN 9781669002871 (pdf) | ISBN 9781669002895 (kindle edition)
Subjects: LCSH: Beyoncé, 1981– —Juvenile literature. | Singers—United States—Biography—Juvenile literature.
Classification: LCC ML3930.K66 S35 2023 (print) | LCC ML3930.K66 (ebook)| DDC 782.42164092 [B]—dc23/eng/20220506
LC record available at https://lccn.loc.gov/2022022115
LC ebook record available at https://lccn.loc.gov/2022022116

Editorial Credits
Editor: Erika L. Shores; Designer: Heidi Thompson; Media Researcher: Jo Miller; Production Specialist: Tori Abraham

All internet sites appearing in back matter were available and accurate when this book was sent to press.

TABLE OF CONTENTS

Words in **bold** are in the glossary.

ALL HAIL QUEEN B

As a famous singer and performer, Beyoncé is full of energy. So, how does she sing and dance without getting tired? When she practices, she runs and sings at the same time. Amazing! It's no wonder she's called Queen B.

What else is there to know about Beyoncé? Read on to learn more!

BEY'S FAVES

So you think you're part of the **Beyhive**?

How many of Beyoncé's favorites do you know?

1. Favorite cereal?

2. Favorite Flower?

3. Favorite cheese?

4. Favorite word?

5. Favorite sport to play?

6. Bonus points for her favorite song to sing in the shower!

1. granola with pecans 2. Blue Vanda orchids

3. cheddar 4. *why* 5. flag football

6. "I Will Always Love You" by Whitney Houston

BEYONCÉ
BY THE NUMBERS

Beyoncé's favorite number is 4. Why?
She was born September 4, 1981, in Houston,
Texas. She married Jay-Z on April 4, 2008.
His birthday is December 4. It would make sense
that Beyoncé named her fourth album 4.

FACT
Beyoncé's full name is Beyoncé
Giselle Knowles-Carter.

Beyoncé's numbers prove she is a megastar. In 2017, she posted a photo on Instagram. She said she was pregnant with twins. The post got 6.3 million likes in less than 8 hours. It was a new Instagram record. By 2022, Beyoncé had won 28 Grammy awards. That's a record for a female singer!

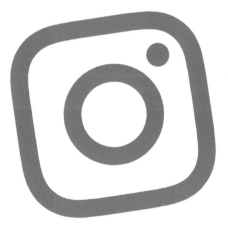

FACT
Beyoncé's seventh studio album came out in 2022. It's titled *Renaissance: Act 1*.

YOUNG 'YONCÉ

Young Bey worked hard to be a great singer and dancer. She began dancing and singing competitions at age 7. As a 9-year-old, she started taking voice lessons. She formed a band called Girl's Tyme. They later changed their name to Destiny's Child.

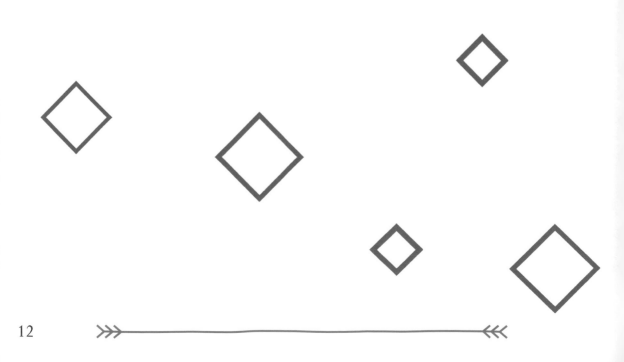

Beyoncé and the other members of Destiny's Child in 1998

Beyoncé was shy when she was growing up. She didn't talk much. She did like to run. Beyoncé would wake up early to run in a park. What else did she do? Every year, she went to the **rodeo** in Houston.

FACT
By age 10, Beyoncé had recorded 50 songs.

△▽△▽△▽△▽△▽△▽△▽△▽

Beyoncé performing in the Houston rodeo

BEYONCÉ'S
WORLD

Beyoncé is still busy as a bee. She has two beehives and about 80,000 bees. For real? Yep! Beyoncé is actually a Queen B. She finds that honey is healthy for her family.

You might think Beyoncé is always glammed up. Not so! At home, she relaxes. She kicks off her high heels. She doesn't wear any makeup. Home time is chill time.

Beyoncé and Jay-Z's home

In 2020, Beyoncé and her kids had Fashion Fridays. They dressed up and took photos. This new habit gave Beyoncé some ideas for her fashion line.

Bey's fashion line is called Ivy Park. Why? She loved to run in the park as a child. Ivy is part of her daughter's name.

FACT

Beyoncé was a part of the remake of *The Lion King* movie. She was the voice of adult Nala.

Blue Ivy and Beyoncé at the movie premiere for *The Lion King*

Beyoncé forgets things, just like anyone. She often misplaces her keys and her phone. Beyoncé says she often forgets to charge her phone too!

Sometimes Beyoncé gets stressed out. How does she relax? Beyoncé prays and **meditates**. She paints. She also relaxes on boats with Jay-Z.

Like lots of people, Beyoncé loves pizza. She often enjoys it on Sundays. Oreo cookies are a favorite treat.

What foods fuel her busy life? Beyoncé likes fish and vegetables. Protein bars and smoothies fill her up too.

^ ^ ^ ^ ^ ^ ^ ^ ^ ^ ^ ^ ^ ^ ^ ^ ^ ^ ^

BEY'S BIG
HEART

Do you know what Bey does with
all her stylish clothes? She saves some
special clothes for her daughters. She also
gives clothes to women in need. How fab
is that?

Bey knows it's important to help others.
She started a program called BeyGood.
It helps people around the world.

SHE'S SO FIERCE

Today, Beyoncé is independent and confident. But she used to be shy and nervous on stage. She decided to create an **alter ego** named Sasha Fierce. Sasha was fearless and bold. Beyoncé acted like Sasha on stage.

Beyoncé doesn't need to act like Sasha Fierce anymore. Beyoncé says she is confident on stage all on her own.

"I'm not happy if I'm not creating, if I'm not dreaming, if I'm not creating a dream and making it into something real ..."
—Beyoncé (*Vogue*, September 2018)

Glossary

alter ego (AWL-tuhr EE-goh)—an alternative self or second self that is different from a person's real personality

Beyhive (BEE-hive)—what Beyoncé's fans are called

meditate (MED-i-tayt)—to relax the mind and body by a regular program of mental exercise

rodeo (ROH-dee-oh)—a contest in which people ride horses and bulls and rope cattle

Read More

Hudd, Emily. *Beyoncé*. North Mankato, MN: Capstone Press, 2020.

Kawa, Katie. *Beyoncé: Making a Difference Through Music*. New York: KidHaven Publishing, 2022.

Warren, Sarah. *Beyoncé: Shine Your Light*. Boston: Houghton Mifflin Harcourt, 2019.

Internet Sites

34 Things You Probably Didn't Know About Beyoncé
insider.com/interesting-things-you-didnt-know-about-beyonce-fun-facts

Beyoncé Official Website
beyonce.com

Inside Beyoncé and Jay-Z's Beautiful Houses
loveproperty.com/gallerylist/100260/inside-Beyoncé-and-jayzs-beautiful-houses

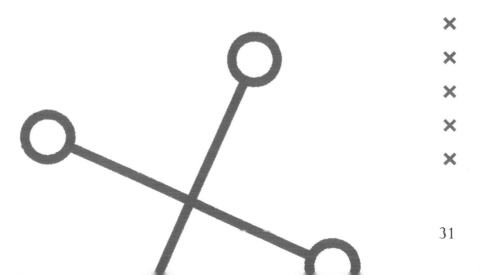

Index

About the Author

Mari Schuh's love of reading began with cereal boxes at the kitchen table. Today she is the author of hundreds of nonfiction books for young readers. Mari lives in the Midwest with her husband and their sassy house rabbit. Learn more about her at marischuh.com.